KNOCK,
KNOCK!

WHO'S
THERE?

A LOAD OF
LAUGHS
AND
JOKES
for kids

KNOCK-KNOCK!
WHO'S THERE?

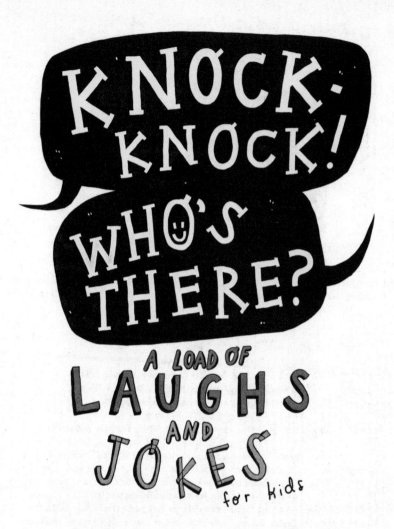

A LOAD OF LAUGHS AND JOKES for kids

Written and drawn by Craig Yoe

LITTLE SIMON
New York London Toronto Sydney New Delhi

LITTLE SIMON
An imprint of Simon & Schuster Children's Publishing Division
1230 Avenue of the Americas, New York, New York 10020
First Little Simon paperback edition May 2018
Copyright © 2018 by Craig Yoe
Portions of this material previously appeared in *The Mighty Big Book of Knock-Knock Jokes*
copyright © 2002 by Craig Yoe
Interior chapter opener photographs copyright © 2018 by Thinkstock
All rights reserved, including the right of reproduction in whole or in part in any form.
LITTLE SIMON is a registered trademark of Simon & Schuster, Inc., and associated
colophon is a trademark of Simon & Schuster, Inc.
For information about special discounts for bulk purchases, please contact
Simon & Schuster Special Sales at 1-866-506-1949 or business@simonandschuster.com.
The Simon & Schuster Speakers Bureau can bring authors to your live event.
For more information or to book an event contact the Simon & Schuster Speakers Bureau
at 1-866-248-3049 or visit our website at www.simonspeakers.com.
Designed by Brittany Naundorff
Manufactured in the United States of America 0318 FFG
2 4 6 8 10 9 7 5 3 1
This book has been cataloged with the Library of Congress.
ISBN 978-1-4814-7820-5 (pbk)   ISBN 978-1-4814-7821-2 (eBook)

To my beloved son and daughter, Griffin and Grace,
and their mama, my *bella* wife, Clizia

Contents

Knock-knock!

Who's there?

Stan!

Stan who?

Standin' here in the rain, can you let me in?

Knock-knock!

Who's there?

Mikey!

Mikey who?

Mikey is in my other pants!

Knock-knock!

Who's there?

Logan!

Logan who?

Logan to your computer, I'll send you an e-mail!

Knock-knock!

Who's there?

Doughnut!

Doughnut who?

Doughnut you wanna open the door and find out?

Knock-knock!

Who's there?

Justin!

Justin who?

Justin time for dinner!

11

Knock-knock!
Who's there?
Danielle!
Danielle who?
Danielle at me!

 **Knock-knock!**
Who's there?
Luke!
Luke who?
Luke through the peephole and find out!

Knock-knock!

Who's there?

Hannah!

Hannah who?

Hannah me the key, quick—I've got to go to the bathroom!

Knock-knock!

Who's there?

Carrie!

Carrie who?

Carrie these groceries for me, will ya?

Knock-knock!

Who's there?

Alexa!

Alexa who?

Alexa to open the door just one more time!

What do you wipe your feet on at a dog lover's house?
A mutt!

CAN YOU GET THAT ?

What do you get when you open the door at Thanksgiving?

A tur-key!

Knock-knock!

Who's there?

Isabelle!

Isabelle who?

Isabelle working or should I keep knocking?

Knock-knock!

Who's there?

Lily!

Lily who?

Lily yay-hee-hoo!

Knock-knock!

Who's there?

Riley!

Riley who?

Riley now, you must know who I am!

Knock-knock!

Who's there?

Megan!

Megan who?

Megan me mad—open the door, already!

YOE!

15

Knock-knock!

Who's there?

Ashley!

Ashley who?

Ashley, never mind!

Knock-knock!

Who's there?

Sara!

Sara who?

Sara doctor in the house?

16

Knock-knock!

Who's there?

Chelsea!

Chelsea who?

Chelsea for yourself if you open the door!

Knock-knock!

Who's there?

Czar!

Czar who?

Czar's gold in them thar hills!

Knock-knock!

Who's there?

Cow!

Cow who?

Cows don't "who," cows go MOOOO!

DOOR SLAMS!

What number is on a ballerina's front door?

2-2!

17

Knock-knock!

Who's there?

Liam!

Liam who?

Liam alone—you're bothering the neighbors with your racket!

Knock-knock!

Who's there?

Jackson!

Jackson who?

Jackson the hill to roll down with Jill!

Knock-knock!

Who's there?

Kerry!

Kerry who?

Kerry me over the threshold!

Knock-knock!

Who's there?

Mary!

Mary who?

Mary me!

Ding Dong!

What sound does a groom's doorbell make?
Ring-ring!

Knock-knock!

Who's there?

Julie!

Julie who?

Julie the key under the mat?

Knock-knock!

Who's there?

Beth!

Beth who?

Beth bet is to open the door and find out!

Knock-knock!

Who's there?

Alex!

Alex who?

Alex-it here—or is this the entrance?

Knock-knock!

Who's there?

Phillip!

Phillip who?

Phillip the candy dish, I've got a sweet tooth!

Knock-knock!

Who's there?

Interrupting cow!

Interr—

MOOOO!

Knock-knock!

Who's there?

Spell!

Spell who?

W-H-O!

Knock-knock!

Who's there?

Annie!

Annie who?

Annie reason in particular you're not letting me in?

Knock-knock!

Who's there?

William!

William who?

William move aside so I can come in?

Knock-knock!

Who's there?

Yah!

Yah who?

What are you so excited about?

Knock-knock!

Who's there?

Lettuce!

Lettuce who?

Lettuce in and you'll find out!

Door Knobbies!

What sign will you find on a plumber's door?

Gone flushing!

Knock-knock!

Who's there?

Abbie!

Abbie who?

Abbie, C, D, E, F, G . . .

Knock-knock!

Who's there?

Olive!

Olive who?

Olive next door—just wanted to say hi!

Knock-knock!

Who's there?

Jason!

Jason who?

Jason the dog down the street!

Knock-knock!

Who's there?

Will!

Will who?

Will you please let me in?

Knock-knock!

Who's there?

Ethan!

Ethan who?

Ethan I know who's there!

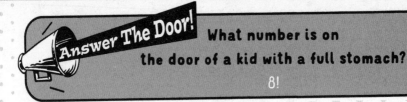

Answer The Door!

What number is on the door of a kid with a full stomach?

8!

Knock-knock!

Who's there?

Yule!

Yule who?

Yule see if you open the door!

Knock-knock!

Who's there?

Bill!

Bill who?

Bill-ieve it or not, it's just me!

Knock-knock!

Who's there?

Adair!

Adair who?

Adair you to find out!

26

Knock-knock!

Who's there?

Allison!

Allison who?

Allison here—you let me in!

Knock-knock!

Who's there?

Anita!

Anita who?

Anita ask you a question—open up!

Knock-knock!

Who's there?

Alfonso!

Alfonso who?

Alfonso you'll know I'm on my way next time!

Knock-knock!

Who's there?

Annette!

Annette who?

Annette is a good thing to fish with!

Knock-knock!

Who's there?

Apollo!

Apollo who?

Apollo-gize for not letting me in!

When a classical musician doesn't use the front door, what door does she use?

The Bach door!

Knock-knock!

Who's there?

Arch!

Arch who?

Arch-n't you gonna let me in?

Knock-knock!

Who's there?

Aretha!

Aretha who?

Aretha is hanging on your door-a!

 **Ding Dong!**

What kind of door does a sleeping person have?
A snore door!

Knock-knock!

Who's there?

Lucy!

Lucy who?

I Lucy my keysie; open the doorsie!

Knock-knock!

Who's there?

Baba!

Baba who?

Baba Black Sheep!

Knock-knock!

Who's there?

Don!

Don who?

Don be silly—you know who it is!

31

Knock-knock!

Who's there?

Al!

Al who?

Al ask the questions here!

Knock-knock!

Who's there?

Ben!

Ben who?

Ben here a while—want to let me in?

Knock-knock!

Who's there?

Boo!

Boo who?

Don't cry; it's only a joke!

Knock-knock!

Who's there?

Emma!

Emma who?

Emma gonna have to knock again, or are you gonna open this door?

Knock-knock!

Who's there?

Bern!

Bern who?

Bern dinner? It smells out here!

Knock-knock!

Who's there?

Caesar!

Caesar who?

Caesars can help you cut things!

Knock-knock!

Who's there?

Cargo!

Cargo who?

Cargo "vroom vroom!"

Knock-knock!

Who's there?

Chantel!

Chantel who?

Chantel ya, sorry!

Door Knobbies!

What kind of door do you find at a

beach house?

A shore door!

Knock-knock!

Who's there?

Cher!

Cher who?

Cher-ing is caring!

Knock-knock!

Who's there?

Carolyn!

Carolyn who?

Christmas Carolyn!

Answer The Door!

What kind of door does a basketball player have?

A score door!

Knock-knock!

Who's there?

Chip!

Chip who?

Chip, Chip, hooray!

Knock-knock!

Who's there?

Charity!

Charity who?

Charity begins at home!

Knock-knock!

Who's there?

Clem!

Clem who?

Clem-bake tonight—wanna come?

Knock-knock!

Who's there?

Walter!

Walter who?

Walter off a duck's back!

Knock-knock!

Who's there?

Courtney!

Courtney who?

Courtney-ds you for jury duty!

Knock-knock!

Who's there?

Dakota!

Dakota who?

Dakota paint is peeling out here!

Knock-knock!

Who's there?

Darwin!

Darwin who?

Darwinning the game 2–1!

Knock-knock!

Who's there?

Dawn!

Dawn who?

Dawn talk to me like that!

Knock-knock!

Who's there?

Aiden!

Aiden who?

Aiden and abettin' since you broke out of jail!

DOOR SLAMS! What kind of door does a monster have?

A gore door!

Knock-knock!

Who's there?

Dewey!

Dewey who?

Dewey have to go through this every time I knock?

Knock-knock!

Who's there?

Diane!

Diane who?

Diane to meet you!

Ding Dong!

What kind of door does a doctor have?
A sore door!

Knock-knock!

Who's there?

Doris!

Doris who?

Doris open—can I come in?

Knock-knock!

Who's there?

Douglas!

Douglas who?

Douglas is half-full!

Knock-knock!

Who's there?

Benjamin!

Benjamin who?

Ben-*jamin* on my guitar!

41

Knock-knock!

Who's there?

Dustin!

Dustin who?

Dustin the wind!

Knock-knock!

Who's there?

Dusty!

Dusty who?

Dusty down here—bring the vacuum!

Knock-knock!

Who's there?

Sophia!

Sophia who?

Sophia and yet so near!

Knock-knock!

Who's there?

Fred!

Fred who?

Fred I can't tell you that!

Knock-knock!

Who's there?

Hugh!

Hugh who?

Hugh mean to tell me you don't know?

Answer The Door!

What kind of door does a pig have?
A boar door!

Knock-knock!

Who's there?

Dutch!

Dutch who?

Bless you!

Knock-knock!

Who's there?

Gabe!

Gabe who?

Gabe all my money to charity!

Knock-knock!

Who's there?

Hal!

Hal who?

Hal should I know?

Knock-knock!

Who's there?

Gladys!

Gladys who?

Gladys me, aren't you?

Knock-knock!

Who's there?

Mia!

Mia who?

Mia key is lost—please open the door!

Knock-knock!

Who's there?

Hank!

Hank who?

You're welcome!

Knock-knock!

Who's there?

Len!

Len who?

Len me five bucks, will ya?

Knock-knock!

Who's there?

Andrew!

Andrew who?

Andrew you a picture—what more do I have to do?

Knock-knock!

Who's there?

Harley!

Harley who?

Harley hear ya; can you speak up?

Knock-knock!

Who's there?

Ari!

Ari who?

Ari-body home?

CAN YOU GET THAT ?

What kind of lock does a barber have on his door?

A lock of hair!

Ding Dong!

What kind of door does a chiropractor have?
A back door!

Knock-knock!

Who's there?

Holden!

Holden who?

Holden my breath until you let me in!

Knock-knock!

Who's there?

Herb!

Herb who?

Herb your dog!

Knock-knock!

Who's there?

Helene!

Helene who?

Helene-d over and kissed me!

48

Knock-knock!

Who's there?

Homer!

Homer who?

Homer's where the heart is!

Knock-knock!

Who's there?

Hope!

Hope who?

Hope you'll let me in soon!

Knock-knock!

Who's there?

Isaiah!

Isaiah who?

Isaiah, dear chap, won't you let me in?

Knock-knock!

Who's there?

Howie!

Howie who?

Howie doing today?

Knock-knock!

Who's there?

Iris!

Iris who?

Iris-ked my life coming over here!

Knock-knock!

Who's there?

Ivana!

Ivana who?

Ivana come in!

Knock-knock!

Who's there?

Matthew!

Matthew who?

Ma-tthew me out of the house, can you let me in?

51

Knock-knock!

Who's there?

Seymour!

Seymour who?

Seymour of me if you let me in!

Knock-knock!

Who's there?

 **Jess!**

Jess who?

I give up, who?

52

Knock-knock!

Who's there?

Addison!

Addison who?

Addison by letting me marry your daughter!

Knock-knock!

Who's there?

Jethro!

Jethro who?

Jethro me a key and I'll let myself in!

Knock-knock!

Who's there?

Jewel!

Jewel who?

Jewel let me in if you know what's good for you!

What number is on Hamlet's door?

2-B (or not 2-B)!

53

Door Knobbies!

What note is on a whale's door?

I'll be humpback in five minutes!

Knock-knock!

Who's there?

Jonah!

Jonah who?

Jonah car or lease one?

Knock-knock!

Who's there?

Judah!

Judah who?

Judah man!

Knock-knock!

Who's there?

Carl!

Carl who?

Carl stall if you don't put gas in it!

54

Knock-knock!

Who's there?

Keegan!

Keegan who?

A Keegan let me in, you know!

Knock-knock!

Who's there?

Banana!

Banana who?

Knock-knock!

Who's there?

Banana!

Banana who?

Knock-knock!

Who's there?

Orange!

Orange who?

Orange you glad I didn't say banana?

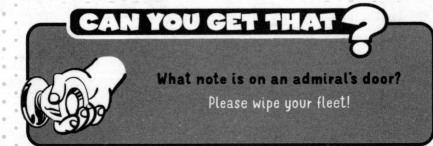

CAN YOU GET THAT?

What note is on an admiral's door?
Please wipe your fleet!

Knock-knock!

Who's there?

Kerry!

Kerry who?

Kerry these bags in for me, please!

Knock-knock!

Who's there?

Zoe!

Zoe who?

Zoe-ven YOU don't recognize me?

Knock-knock!

Who's there?

Lacey!

Lacey who?

Lacey good-for-nothing!

Knock-knock!

Who's there?

Keisha!

Keisha who?

Keisha would come in handy right now!

Ding Dong!

What does it sound like when you
knock on Frankenstein's door?
Shock! Shock!

Knock-knock!

Who's there?

Kenya!

Kenya who?

Kenya come out and play?

Knock-knock!

Who's there?

Mae!

Mae who?

Mae I please come in?

Knock-knock!

Who's there?

Caden!

Caden who?

Caden you please let me in?

59

Knock-knock!

Who's there?

Malcolm!

Malcolm who?

Malcolms from the post office!

Knock-knock!

Who's there?

Mark!

Mark who?

Mark my words, I'll be back!

Knock-knock!

Who's there?

Kent!

Kent who?

Kent reach the doorbell—that's why I'm knocking!

Knock-knock!

Who's there?

Martian!

Martian who?

Martian band!

Knock-knock!

Who's there?

Mary Lee!

Mary Lee who?

**Mary Lee, Mary Lee, Mary Lee, Mary Lee,
life is but a dream!**

Knock-knock!

Who's there?

Ryan!

Ryan who?

Ryan you makin' me knock so much?

Knock-knock!

Who's there?

 **Max!**

Max who?

Max sure you let me in!

Knock-knock!

Who's there?

Miranda!

Miranda who?

Miranda the store to get some milk!

Knock-knock!

Who's there?

Alexander!

Alexander who?

Alexander friend are coming up the steps!

Knock-knock!

Who's there?

Misty!

Misty who?

Misty bus, so give me a ride!

Knock-knock!

Who's there?

Macy!

Macy who?

Macy some ID?

Door Knobbies!

What does it sound like when you
knock on a dressmaker's door?

Frock! Frock!

Knock-knock!

Who's there?

Nathan!

Nathan who?

Nathan new with me; what's new with you?

Knock-knock!

Who's there?

Nicholas!

Nicholas who?

Nicholas less than a dime. Open the door and

I'll give you my time!

Knock-knock!

Who's there?

Newt!

Newt who?

Newt to town. Can you show me around?

Knock-knock!

Who's there?

Nicole!

Nicole who?

Nicole for your thoughts (I don't have a penny)!

Knock-knock!

Who's there?

Cindy!

Cindy who?

Cindy the butler to open the door!

CAN YOU GET THAT ?

What's the trick to walking through walls?

Use the door!

Knock-knock!

Who's there?

Nita!

Nita who?

Nita key!

Knock-knock!

Who's there?

Noah!

Noah who?

Noah good restaurant around here?

Knock-knock!

Who's there?

Albie!

Albie who?

Albie back!

Knock-knock!

Who's there?

Adele!

Adele who?

Adele-icate situation!

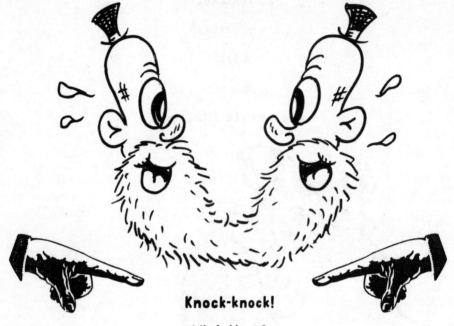

Knock-knock!

Who's there?

Amy!

Amy who?

Amy-body home?

Knock-knock!

Who's there?

L. B.!

L. B. who?

L. B. seeing you!

70

Knock-knock!

Who's there?

Agatha!

Agatha who?

Agatha go right now, I'll see ya later!

Knock-knock!

Who's there?

Rita!

Rita who?

Rita good book lately?

Knock-knock!

Who's there?

Pat!

Pat who?

Pat me on the back as I just won a medal!

What is orange and goes "slam, slam, slam, slam"?
A four-door carrot!

Knock-knock!

Who's there?

Russ!

Russ who?

Russ Pilaf!

72

What did the man say when he knocked on the museum door?

"Show me the Monet!"

Knock-knock!

Who's there?

Ron!

Ron who?

Ron, Ron as fast as you can!

You can't catch me, I'm the Gingerbread Man!

Knock-knock!

Who's there?

Gorilla!

Gorilla who?

Gorilla your dreams!

Knock-knock!

Who's there?

Elijah!

Elijah who?

Elijah self down, take a nap, then answer the door!

73

Knock-knock!

Who's there?

Zelda!

Zelda who?

Zelda house, we're moving!

Knock-knock!

Who's there?

Far East!

Far East who?

Far East a jolly good fellow!

Knock-knock!

Who's there?

Mac!

Mac who?

Mac my day!

Knock-knock!

Who's there?

Annette!

Annette who?

Annette-a day, Annette-a dollar!

75

Knock-knock!

Who's there?

Mabel!

Mabel who?

Mabel syrup!

Knock-knock!

Who's there?

Etta!

Etta who?

**Etta something that didn't agree with me,
I think I'm gonna barf!**

Knock-knock!

Who's there?

Nana!

Nana who?

Nana your business!

Knock-knock!

Who's there?

Eubie!

Eubie who?

Eubie long in a zoo!

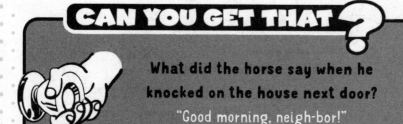

CAN YOU GET THAT ?

What did the horse say when he
knocked on the house next door?

"Good morning, neigh-bor!"

Knock-knock!

Who's there?

Barry!

Barry who?

Barry nice to meet you!

Knock-knock!

Who's there?

Noah!

Noah who?

Noah business like show business!

Knock-knock!

Who's there?

Olive!

Olive who?

Olive you! Open the door and give me a kiss!

Knock-knock!

Who's there?

Nemo!

Nemo who?

Nemo money!

Knock-knock!

Who's there?

Newt!

Newt who?

Newt Jersey is the Garden State!

Knock-knock!

Who's there?

Olga!

Olga who?

Olga phone, I'll be right there!

What color is Dracula's door?
Ghoul-den!

Knock-knock!

Who's there?

Shelley!

Shelley who?

Shelley have a game of tennis?

Knock-knock!

Who's there?

Kansas!

Kansas who?

Kansas be Friday already?

Knock-knock!

Who's there?

Joshua!

Joshua who?

Joshua doggone minute there and let me in!

81

What do you say when Santa opens the door?
"Yo ho ho ho!"

Knock-knock!

Who's there?

Iowa!

Iowa who?

Iowa ten dollars; I'm here to pay!

Knock-knock!

Who's there?

Missouri!

Missouri who?

Missouri loves company!

Knock-knock!

Who's there?

Vera!

Vera who?

Vera do you keep the keys?

82

Knock-knock!

Who's there?

Milo!

Milo who?

Milo-wer back itches, please scratch it!

83

Knock-knock!

Who's there?

Sandro!

Sandro who?

Sandro children out to play!

Knock-knock!

Who's there?

Jen!

Jen who?

Jen in Rome, do as the Romans do!

Knock-knock!

Who's there?

Denny!

Denny who?

Denny bone's connected to the leg bone!

Knock-knock!

Who's there?

Alma!

Alma who?

Alma the one knocking on the door!

Knock-knock!

Who's there?

Claudia!

Claudia who?

Claudia doctor, I'm sick!

Knock-knock!

Who's there?

Alda!

Alda who?

Alda people in the world and you had to answer the door!

Knock-knock!

Who's there?

Riley!

Riley who?

Riley cold out here, let me in!

Knock-knock!

Who's there?

Agatha!

Agatha who?

Agatha get out of this place!

What do you say when a florist opens the door?

"How's your mum?"

Knock-knock!

Who's there?

Willis!

Willis who?

Willis pants fit me?

Knock-knock!

Who's there?

Reggie!

Reggie who?

Reggie or not, here I come!

Knock-knock!

Who's there?

Celeste!

Celeste who?

Celeste time I'm gonna tell you!

Knock-knock!

Who's there?

Emily!

Emily who?

Emily-ving for the beach—wanna come?

Knock-knock!

Who's there?

Jesse!

Jesse who?

Jesse through the peephole!

Door Knobbies!

What do you say when a garbage collector opens the door?

"Can I come in?"

Knock-knock!

Who's there?

Gil!

Gil who?

Gil-ty as charged!

Knock-knock!

Who's there?

Ozzie!

Ozzie who?

Ozzie your house is for sale!

Knock-knock!

Who's there?

Aaron!

Aaron who?

Aaron you glad to see me?

Knock-knock!

Who's there?

Tori!

Tori who?

Tori back of my pants—let me in!

Knock-knock!

Who's there?

Canoe!

Canoe who?

Canoe keep it down? I have a headache!

Knock-knock!

Who's there?

Kurt!

Kurt who?

I Kurt myself—can you kelp me?

92

Knock-knock!

Who's there?

Jacob!

Jacob who?

Jacob and get out of bed!

Knock-knock!

Who's there?

John!

John who?

John hands and make a circle!

Knock-knock!

Who's there?

Griffin!

Griffin who?

Griff-in, but Grace out!

What do you say when a dentist opens the door?

"How are you filling today?"

What do you say when a teacher opens the door?
"You've got class!"

Knock-knock!
Who's there?
Althea!
Althea who?
Althea later, alligator!

Knock-knock!
Who's there?
Juan!
Juan who?
Juan day at a time!

Knock-knock!
Who's there?
Gorilla!
Gorilla who?
Gorilla some hamburgers!

94

Knock-knock!

Who's there?

Pisa!

Pisa who?

Pisa cake!

Knock-knock!

Who's there?

Brina!

Brina who?

Brina key to the door!

Knock-knock!

Who's there?

Andrea!

Andrea who?

Andrea-ming of a white Christmas!

Knock-knock!

Who's there?

Art!

Art who?

Art for art's sake!

Knock-knock!

Who's there?

Alfred!

Alfred who?

Alfred I'll have to get back to you on that one!

Knock-knock!

Who's there?

Dennis!

Dennis who?

Dennis says I have to get my teeth cleaned!

Knock-knock!

Who's there?

Sal!

Sal who?

Sal and pepper!

Knock-knock!

Who's there?

Xena!

Xena who?

Xena good movie lately?

Knock-knock!

Who's there?

Raina!

Raina who?

Raina, Raina go away—come again another day!

CAN YOU GET THAT?

What do you say when a foot doctor opens the door?

"Nice toe meet you!"

Knock-knock!

Who's there?

Howard!

Howard who?

I'm fine, Howard you?

Knock-knock!

Who's there?

Hugo!

Hugo who?

Hugo girl!

Knock-knock!

Who's there?

Fred!

Fred who?

Fred of my own shadow!

Door Knobbies!

What do you say when a car mechanic opens the door?

"You auto get your doorbell fixed!"

Knock-knock!

Who's there?

Phil!

Phil who?

Phil it up with regular!

Knock-knock!

Who's there?

Brad!

Brad who?

Brad and butter!

Knock-knock!

Who's there?

Curt!

Curt who?

Don't be Curt with me!

Knock-knock!

Who's there?

Darius!

Darius who?

Darius a right way and a wrong way!

Knock-knock!

Who's there?

Custer!

Custer who?

Custer or cream cheese?

Knock-knock!

Who's there?

Coupon!

Coupon who?

Coupon truckin'!

What do you say when a farmer opens the door?

"Plow are you?"

Knock-knock!

Who's there?

Abigail!

Abigail who?

Abigail friend with me, can we come in?

Knock-knock!

Who's there?

Harry!

Harry who?

Harry up and open the door!

Ding Dong!

**What do you say when
a shepherd opens the door?**
"Nice to meet ewe!"

Knock-knock!

Who's there?

Carmen!

Carmen who?

Carmen to my arms and give me a hug!

Knock-knock!

Who's there?

Toby!

Toby who?

Toby or not Toby?

Knock-knock!

Who's there?

Ivan!

Ivan who?

Ivan the lottery!

Knock-knock!

Who's there?

Joy!

Joy who?

Joy to the world!

Knock-knock!

Who's there?

Dennis!

Dennis who?

Dennis anyone?

Knock-knock!

Who's there?

Carl!

Carl who?

Carl be here to pick us up soon!

Knock-knock!

Who's there?

Yukon!

Yukon who?

Yukon lead a horse to water, but you can't make him drink!

Knock-knock!

Who's there?

Iris!

Iris who?

Iris you would open the door!

 What sign does a car mechanic have
on his door?
No auto-body's home!

Knock-knock!

Who's there?

Izzy!

Izzy who?

Izzy for you to say!

Knock-knock!

Who's there?

Hackensack!

Hackensack who?

Hackensack it to ya!

Knock-knock!

Who's there?

Alfie!

Alfie who?

Alfie you in court!

108

Knock-knock!

Who's there?

Fern!

Fern who?

Fern crying out loud, let me in!

Knock-knock!

Who's there?

Earl!

Earl who?

Earl let you know!

110

Knock-knock!

Who's there?

Manny!

Manny who?

Manny are called; few are chosen!

Knock-knock!

Who's there?

Nathan!

Nathan who?

Nathan but the best for you!

Knock-knock!

Who's there?

Marilyn!

Marilyn who?

Marilyn we roll along!

Door Knobbies!

What do you say when an optometrist opens the door?

"Nice to see you!"

Knock-knock!

Who's there?

Noah!

Noah who?

Noah parking on the left side of the street!

Knock-knock!

Who's there?

Tennis!

Tennis who?

Tennis the number that comes after nine!

Knock-knock!

Who's there?

Hugh!

Hugh who?

Hugh don't want to know!

Knock-knock!

Who's there?

Cashew!

Cashew who?

Cashew see I'm freezing out here?

Knock-knock!

Who's there?

 **Patty!**

Patty who?

Patty melt on rye!

Knock-knock!

Who's there?

Troy!

Troy who?

Troy, Troy again!

Knock-knock!

Who's there?

Darryl!

Darryl who?

Darryl be a new moon tonight!

Knock-knock!

Who's there?

Fur!

Fur who?

Fur the last time—open the door!

Knock-knock!

Who's there?

Cash!

Cash who?

Cash is what you need to buy things!

What do you do when Dracula
opens the door?

"Fangs for letting me in!"

Ding Dong!

What do you say when you knock on a scale's door?

"I've been weighting here for hours!"

Knock-knock!

Who's there?

Donna!

Donna who?

Donna you wanna lemme in?

Knock-knock!

Who's there?

Inez!

Inez who?

Inez-er answer such stupid questions!

Knock-knock!

Who's there?

Harry!

Harry who?

Harry armpits!

Knock-knock!

Who's there?

Ilene!

Ilene who?

Ilene against the door till you open up!

Knock-knock!

Who's there?

Esther!

Esther who?

Esther Bunny!

Knock-knock!

Who's there?

Butch!

Butch who?

Butch your money where your mouth is!

Knock-knock!

Who's there?

Colleen!

Colleen who?

Colleen all cars! Colleen all cars!

Knock-knock!

Who's there?

Opportunity!

Opportunity who?

Opportunity knocks but once!

Knock-knock!

Who's there?

Atlas!

Atlas who?

Atlas I've come knocking at your door!

119

Knock-knock!

Who's there?

Isadore!

Isadore who?

Isadore locked?

Knock-knock!

Who's there?

Dylan!

Dylan who?

Dylan cards—want to play a game?

Knock-knock!

Who's there?

Justice!

Justice who?

Justice I suspected!

Answer The Door!

What do you say when a
computer geek opens the door?

"How's your ROM?"

Knock-knock!

Who's there?

Cheri!

Cheri who?

Cheri-o, old chap!

Knock-knock!

Who's there?

Jon!

Jon who?

Jon fishing!

Knock-knock!

Who's there?

Karen!

Karen who?

Karen heavy boxes—can you open the door?

122

Knock-knock!

Who's there?

Leif!

Leif who?

Leif me alone!

Knock-knock!

Who's there?

Trace!

Trace who?

Trace-ing my steps—I lost something!

Door Knobbies!

What do you say when a cheerleader opens the door?
"How's your pom-pom?"

Knock-knock!

Who's there?

Darren!

Darren who?

Darren you to come to the door and find out!

Knock-knock!

Who's there?

Joan!

Joan who?

Joan let the bedbugs bite!

Knock-knock!

Who's there?

Allen!

Allen who?

Allen-eed is love!

Knock-knock!

Who's there?

Pat!

Pat who?

Pat the dog—he's bringing in the newspaper!

Knock-knock!

Who's there?

Ella!

Ella who?

Ella-lujah! Someone's home!

Knock-knock!

Who's there?

Pearl!

Pearl who?

Pearl chance I'll tell you if you open the door!

Knock-knock!

Who's there?

Alan!

Alan who?

Alan you ten dollars, now you've got to pay me back!

Knock-knock!

Who's there?

Luke!

Luke who?

Luke what the cat dragged in!

Knock-knock!

Who's there?

Jane Telman!

Jane Telman who?

Jane Telman and ladies!

129

Knock-knock!

Who's there?

Eva!

Eva who?

Eva-ry dark cloud has a silver lining!

Knock-knock!

Who's there?

Dewey!

Dewey who?

Dewey have to ask? I'm your mother!

Knock-knock!

Who's there?

Kendall!

Kendall who?

Kendall in the wind!

Knock-knock!

Who's there?

New Year!

New Year who?

New Year were gonna ask me that!

What do you say when a rabbit opens the door?

"Thanks fur letting me in!"

DOOR SLAMS!

What do you say when you knock on a baker's door?
"Open sesame!"

Knock-knock!

Who's there?

Tish!

Tish who?

Yes, thanks, my nose is running!

Knock-knock!

Who's there?

Harry and Gavin!

Harry and Gavin who?

Harry today, Gavin tomorrow!

Knock-knock!

Who's there?

Esther!

Esther who?

Esther a way I can get in?

Knock-knock!

Who's there?

Nanette!

Nanette who?

Need Nanette to go fishing with!

Knock-knock!

Who's there?

Bear!

Bear who?

Bear with me—do you have some honey?

Knock-knock!

Who's there?

Jimmy!

Jimmy who?

Jimmy a break!

Ding Dong!

What do you say when an antique dealer opens the door?
"What's new?"

Knock-knock!

Who's there?

Rich!

Rich who?

Rich way did they go?

Knock-knock!

Who's there?

Dana!

Dana who?

Dana talk to me like that!

Knock-knock!

Who's there?

Dinah!

Dinah who?

Dinah-saur!

135

Knock-knock!

Who's there?

Bonnie!

Bonnie who?

Bonnie rabbit!

Knock-knock!

Who's there?

Carrie!

Carrie who?

Carrie me back home!

Knock-knock!

Who's there?

Don Juan!

Don Juan who?

Don Juan to keep knocking—open the door!

Knock-knock!

Who's there?

Ivan!

Ivan who?

Ivan no way of knowing! I was hoping you could tell me!

137

Door Knobbies!

What does a housekeeper use to keep her door open?

A door mop!

Knock-knock!

Who's there?

Carlos!

Carlos who?

Carlos a tire, do you have a spare?

Knock-knock!

Who's there?

Donna!

Donna who?

Donna ever change; I love you just the way you are!

Knock-knock!

Who's there?

Hazel!

Hazel who?

Hazel-long, I'll be seeing you!

Knock-knock!

Who's there?

Hugh!

Hugh who?

Hugh let the dogs out?

Knock-knock!

Who's there?

Ezra!

Ezra who?

Ezra anybody home?

Knock-knock!

Who's there?

Homer!

Homer who?

Homer, Homer on the range!

Knock-knock!

Who's there?

Isaiah!

Isaiah who?

Isaiah nothing without my lawyer!

Knock-knock!

Who's there?

I've often wondered that myself. . . .

CAN YOU GET THAT?

What does a pig use to
keep his door open?

A door slop!

Ding Dong!

What does it sound like when you knock on a bird's door?
Hawk! Hawk!

Knock-knock!

Who's there?

Arnold!

Arnold who?

Arnold worn-out shoe!

Knock-knock!

Who's there?

Ashley!

Ashley who?

Ashley, I don't really know!

Knock-knock!

Who's there?

Reba!

Reba who?

Reba good book lately?

Knock-knock!

Who's there?

Aurora!

Aurora who?

Aurora is the sound a lion makes!

Knock-knock!

Who's there?

Ivana!

Ivana who?

Ivana my mama!

Knock-knock!

Who's there?

Merle!

Merle who?

Merle, Merle! It's your little kitty cat!

Knock-knock!

Who's there?

Oprah!

Oprah who?

**Oprah the river and through the woods,
to Grandmother's house we go!**

Knock-knock!

Who's there?

Wayne!

Wayne who?

Wayne are you gonna open the door?

Knock-knock!

Who's there?

Bridget!

Bridget who?

Bridget over troubled water!

Knock-knock!

Who's there?

Betty!

Betty who?

Betty fix your doorbell, I had to use the knocker!

Knock-knock!

Who's there?

Shirley!

Shirley who?

Shirley you'll open the door!

Knock-knock!

Who's there?

Kip!

Kip who?

Kip out!

What does a farmer use to keep his door open?

A door crop!

Knock-knock!

Who's there?

Hugo!

Hugo who?

Hugo fly a kite!

147

Knock-knock!

Who's there?

Don!

Don who?

Don talk back!

 **Answer The Door!**
**What do you say
when a buffalo opens the door?**
"What's gnu?"

Knock-knock!

Who's there?

Toucan!

Toucan who?

Toucan live cheaper than one!

Knock-knock!

Who's there?

Bella!

Bella who?

Bella button!

Knock-knock!

Who's there?

Donovan!

Donovan who?

Donovan go there!

Knock-knock!

Who's there?

Alma!

Alma who?

Alma love!

Knock-knock!

Who's there?

Olive and Olive!

Olive and Olive who?

Olive and Olive and I'll blow your house down!

What does a bunny use to keep her door open?
A door hop!

Knock-knock!

Who's there?

Frank Lee!

Frank Lee who?

Frank Lee, my dear, I don't give a darn!

Knock-knock!

Who's there?

Thelma!

Thelma who?

Thelma box is full; pick up your letters!

Ding Dong!

**What does a dad
use to keep his door open?**
A door pop!

Knock-knock!

Who's there?

Cash!

Cash who?

Are you calling me a nut?!

Knock-knock!

Who's there?

Becca!

Becca who?

Becca up, I'm coming in!

Knock-knock!

Who's there?

Bob!

Bob who?

Bob-ing for apples!

Knock-knock!

Who's there?

Theresa!

Theresa who?

Theresa new moon rising!

Knock-knock!

Who's there?

Gerald!

Gerald who?

Gerald Grandpappy!

Knock-knock!

Who's there?

Montel!

Montel who?

Montel-ephone is ringing, and I've got to answer it!

Knock-knock!

Who's there?

Justin!

Justin who?

This Justin ... man bites dog!

Knock-knock!

Who's there?

Yvette!

Yvette who?

Yvette my candy bar—you owe me a dollar!

155

Door Knobbies!

What door does a comedian knock on when he's sick?

The door to the he-he-mergency room!

Knock-knock!

Who's there?

Jess!

Jess who?

Jess call me Jess!

Knock-knock!

Who's there?

Colby!

Colby who?

Colby tomorrow; today I hab a cold!

Knock-knock!

Who's there?

Ida!

Ida who?

Ida rather be skiing!

156

Knock-knock!

Who's there?

Uriah and Uriah!

Uriah and Uriah who?

Uriahs are beautiful!

Knock-knock!

Who's there?

Vaughn!

Vaughn who?

Vaughn, two, buckle my shoe!

Knock-knock!

Who's there?

Nora!

Nora who?

Nora way am I gonna tell you!

Knock-knock!

Who's there?

Willa!

Willa who?

Willa you open the door?

Knock-knock!

Who's there?

Yvonne!

Yvonne who?

Yvonne me to come in now?

Knock-knock!

Who's there?

Jimmy!

Jimmy who?

Jimmy the lock!

Knock-knock!

Who's there?

Lindy!

Lindy who?

Lindy me a cup of sugar, please!

Knock-knock!

Who's there?

Athena!

Athena who?

Athena ghost!

What does a karate expert use to keep his door open?

A door chop!

Knock-knock!

Who's there?

Warren!

Warren who?

Warren peace!

161

Knock-knock!

Who's there?

Candy!

Candy who?

Candy kids come out to play with me?

162

Knock-knock!

Who's there?

Cassandra!

Cassandra who?

Cassandra mother will give you a time-out!

Knock-knock!

Who's there?

Bailey!

Bailey who?

Bailey hear ya—can you speak up?

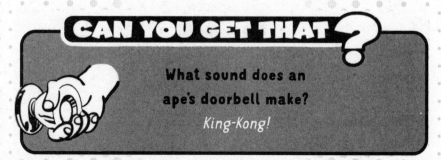

CAN YOU GET THAT ?

What sound does an ape's doorbell make?

King-Kong!

**What sound does a
music teacher's doorbell make?**
Sing-song!

Knock-knock!

Who's there?

Collier!

Collier who?

Collier sister—I'm here for our date!

Knock-knock!

Who's there?

Leslie!

Leslie who?

Leslie the door open next time so I can walk right in!

Knock-knock!

Who's there?

Freddie!

Freddie who?

Freddie or not, here I come!

164

 **Knock-knock!**

Who's there?

Maria!

Maria who?

Maria name is Flootersnoot, but you can call me Flootie!

Knock-knock!

Who's there?

Morgan!

Morgan who?

Morgan you can handle—I brought the whole family!

Knock-knock!

Who's there?

Emma!

Emma who?

Emma ever gonna get in?

Knock-knock!

Who's there?

Brooke!

Brooke who?

Brooke my leg skiing—can you help me through the door?

Knock-knock!

Who's there?

Amber!

Amber who?

Amber-ping and belching out here!

CAN YOU GET THAT

**What sound does a
table-tennis player's doorbell make?**
Ping-pong!

Knock-knock!

Who's there?

Sam!

Sam who?

Sam old, Sam old!

Knock-knock!

Who's there?

Shelby!

Shelby who?

Shelby comin' around the mountain when she comes!

Knock-knock!

Who's there?

Alec!

Alec who?

Alec ice cream—don't you?

168

Knock-knock!

Who's there?

Norm!

Norm who?

Norm-ally these jokes are much funnier than this!

Knock-knock!

Who's there?

Owls go!

Owls go who?

That's right, they do!

170

Knock-knock!

Who's there?

Samantha!

Samantha who?

Samantha see about the plumbing!

Knock-knock!

Who's there?

Ali!

Ali who?

Ali, Ali oxen free!

Knock-knock!

Who's there?

Justin!

Justin who?

Justin Case!

Ding Dong!

What sound does a bee's doorbell make?

Sting-stong!

When is a door obnoxious?
When it's spelled backward!

Knock-knock!

Who's there?

Ira!

Ira who?

Ira-n away from a bee!

Knock-knock!

Who's there?

Erin!

Erin who?

Erin boy—I got your packages!

Knock-knock!

Who's there?

Wilma!

Wilma who?

Wilma ship ever come in?

Knock-knock!

Who's there?

Amanda!

Amanda who?

Amanda hug and kiss!

Knock-knock!

Who's there?

Grace!

Grace who?

Grace me with your presence, Papa, Griffin, and Mama, and let me in!

Knock-knock!

Who's there?

Anna!

Anna who?

Anna one, Anna two . . .

Knock-knock!

Who's there?

Hailey!

Hailey who?

Hailey me a taxi, please!

Ding Dong!

What are movie actors' doors made of?

Holly-wood!

Knock-knock!

Who's there?

Alex!

Alex who?

Alex my mama, I forget!

Knock-knock!

Who's there?

Ida!

Ida who?

Ida know!

Knock-knock!

Who's there?

Mya!

Mya who?

Mya sugar bowl is empty—can I borrow a cup?

Knock-knock!

Who's there?

Major!

Major who?

Major look!

177

Knock-knock!

Who's there?

Cass!

Cass who?

Cass your care upon the water!

What are most doors made of?
Wood-n't you like to know?

Knock-knock!

Who's there?

Watson!

Watson who?

Watson the table? I'm hungry!

Knock-knock!

Who's there?

Noah!

Noah who?

Noah thyself!

Knock-knock!

Who's there?

Orange!

Orange who?

Orange you going to let me in?

179

Knock-knock!

Who's there?

Francie!

Francie who?

Francie meeting you here!

Knock-knock!

Who's there?

July!

July who?

July like a rug!

Knock-knock!

Who's there?

Little Old Lady!

Little Old Lady who?

I didn't know you could yodel!

Knock-knock!

Who's there?

Olivia!

Olivia who?

Olivia me alone!

183

CAN YOU GET THAT ?

What's a thief's door made of?
Steel!

Knock-knock!

Who's there?

Eddie!

Eddie who?

Eddie-body home?

Knock-knock!

Who's there?

Bruce!

Bruce who?

I Bruce some tea and brought it over!

Knock-knock!

Who's there?

Disguise!

Disguise who?

Disguise are cloudy; can I borrow your umbrella?

Knock-knock!

Who's there?

Omar!

Omar who?

Omar goodness, I forgot my key!

Knock-knock!

Who's there?

 **Sadie!**

Sadie who?

Sadie magic word and I'll tell you!

Knock-knock!

Who's there?

Wendy!

Wendy who?

Wendy you think you'll open the door?

Knock-knock!

Who's there?

Igor!

Igor who?

Igor to talk to you! Let me in!

Knock-knock!

Who's there?

Anita!

Anita who?

Anita you to let me in!

Knock-knock!

Who's there?

Jamaica!

Jamaica who?

Jamaica me sick!

DOOR SLAMS!

What's a sheep thief's door made of?

Steel wool!

 What looks like a door, feels like a door, and smells like a door?

A door!

Knock-knock!

Who's there?

Pitcher!

Pitcher who?

Pitcher arms around me!

Knock-knock!

Who's there?

Raina!

Raina who?

Raina check!

Knock-knock!

Who's there?

Morris!

Morris who?

Morris less and less is more!

Knock-knock!

Who's there?

Thermos!

Thermos who?

Thermos be a reason you won't let me in,

but I can't figure it out!

Knock-knock!

Who's there?

Nancy!

Nancy who?

Nancy meeting you here!

Knock-knock!

Who's there?

Marcella!

Marcella who?

Marcella is at the bottom of my house!

Knock-knock!

Who's there?

Stan!

Stan who?

Stan back, I'm gonna kick the door down!

Knock-knock!

Who's there?

Shemp!

Shemp who?

Shemp who is what you wash your hair with!

Knock-knock!

Who's there?

Sid!

Sid who?

Sid down and rest awhile!

Knock-knock!

Who's there?

Vera!

Vera who?

Vera rude of you not to let me in!

192

Knock-knock!

Who's there?

Zany!

Zany who?

Zany-body in there?

Knock-knock!

Who's there?

Yacht!

Yacht who?

Yacht not ask so many questions!

Knock-knock!

Who's there?

Xavier!

Xavier who?

Xavier breath; I won't answer your questions!

Knock-knock!

Who's there?

Tamara!

Tamara who?

Tamara is another day!

194

Ding Dong!

What day will a chicken not open his door?
Fry-day!

Knock-knock!

Who's there?

Alma!

Alma who?

Alma woman of mystery!

Knock-knock!

Who's there?

Snow!

Snow who?

Snow ice-skating today!

Knock-knock!

Who's there?

Nicholas!

Nicholas who?

Nicholas four cents more than a penny!

195

Knock-knock!

Who's there?

Wade!

Wade who?

Wade'll I get inside!

Knock-knock!

Who's there?

Walter!

Walter who?

Walter you asking so many questions for?

What day will Frosty the Snowman not open his door?

Sun-day!

Knock-knock!

Who's there?

Warrior!

Warrior who?

Warrior been? I've been knocking for hours!

197

Knock-knock!

Who's there?

Weasel!

Weasel who?

Weasel be back if you don't let us in!

Ding Dong!

What does it sound like when you knock on a seagull's door?
Flock! Flock!

Knock-knock!

Who's there?

Moe!

Moe who?

Moe your lawn for ten dollars!

Knock-knock!

Who's there?

Wanda!

Wanda who?

Wanda let me in now?

Knock-knock!

Who's there?

Icy!

Icy who?

Icy no reason for not letting me in!

199

Knock-knock!

Who's there?

Sherwood!

Sherwood who?

Sherwood like to come in!

Knock-knock!

Who's there?

Dismay!

Dismay who?

Dismay seem funny, but I'm not laughing!

Knock-knock!

Who's there?

Teresa!

Teresa who?

**Teresa reason why you're not letting me in,
but I don't know what it is!**

Knock-knock!

Who's there?

Ice cream!

Ice cream who?

Ice cream if you don't let me in!

Knock-knock!

Who's there?

Twyla!

Twyla who?

Twyla heck won't you let me in?

Knock-knock!

Who's there?

Alastair!

Alastair who?

Alastair at you until you let me in!

Knock-knock!

Who's there?

Aaron!

Aaron who?

Aaron the side of caution!

What day do you open your door twice?
Two-sday!

Knock-knock!

Who's there?

Boyd!

Boyd who?

Boyd sure like to come in!

Knock-knock!

Who's there?

Attila!

Attila who?

Attila your mother if you don't let me in!

Knock-knock!

Who's there?

Andy!

Andy who?

Andy dish ran away with the spoon!

Knock-knock!

Who's there?

Warner!

Warner who?

Warner go to a movie with me?

Knock-knock!

Who's there?

Drew!

Drew who?

Drew you a picture; want to see it?

Knock-knock!

Who's there?

Andrew!

Andrew who?

Andrew you one too!

205

Knock-knock!

Who's there?

Leda!

Leda who?

Leda horse to water but you can't make it drink!

Knock-knock!

Who's there?

Annapolis!

Annapolis who?

Annapolis a day keeps the doctor away!

Knock-knock!

Who's there?

Mama!

Mama who?

Mama said there'd be days like this!

Knock-knock!

Who's there?

Izzy!

Izzy who?

Izzy as pie!

Knock-knock!

Who's there?

Cole!

Cole who?

Cole your mother!

Knock-knock!

Who's there?

Count!

Count who?

Count-ing the minutes!

Knock-knock!

Who's there?

Moore!

Moore who?

Moore powerful than a locomotive!

Knock-knock!

Who's there?

Bea!

Bea who?

Bea in your bonnet!

Ding Dong!

What country do doors come from?
Ecua-door!

Knock-knock!

Who's there?

Al!

Al who?

Al-phabet soup!

Knock-knock!

Who's there?

Stan!

Stan who?

Stan pat!

Knock-knock!

Who's there?

Kelli!

Kelli who?

Kelli-fornia, here I come!

Knock-knock!

Who's there?

Maura!

Maura who?

Maura less!

Knock-knock!

Who's there?

Gopher!

Gopher who?

Gopher broke!

Knock-knock!

Who's there?

Rose!

Rose who?

Rose, Rose, Rose your boat!

Knock-knock!

Who's there?

Duane!

Duane who?

Duane the bathtub—I'm dwowning!

Knock-knock!

Who's there?

Grant!

Grant who?

Grant and bear it!

Knock-knock!

Who's there?

Bernice!

Bernice who?

Bernice the midnight oil!

Knock-knock!

Who's there?

Bella!

Bella who?

Bella cherries!

Knock-knock!

Who's there?

Midas!

Midas who?

Midas well tell you the truth: I'm not Midas, I'm Patricia!

Knock-knock!

Who's there?

Dale!

Dale who?

Dale me in!

Door Knobbies!

What kind of door does a cheater have?

A scheme door!

Knock-knock!

Who's there?

Rhea!

Rhea who?

Rhea my lips!

Knock-knock!

Who's there?

Paul!

Paul who?

Paul yourself up by your bootstraps!

Knock-knock!

Who's there?

Celia!

Celia who?

Celia around!

Knock-knock!

Who's there?

Cain!

Cain who?

Cain of worms!

CAN YOU GET THAT ?

**What kind of door
does a dry cleaner have?**
A steam door!

Knock-knock!

Who's there?

Dawn!

Dawn who?

Dawn worry, be happy!

Knock-knock!

Who's there?

Doughnut!

Doughnut who?

Doughnut be your own worst enemy!

Knock-knock!

Who's there?

Wayne!

Wayne who?

Wayne the going gets tough, the tough get going!

Knock-knock!

Who's there?

Wayne!

Wayne who?

Wayne the cows come home!

Knock-knock!

Who's there?

Wayne!

Wayne who?

Wayne life gives you lemons, make lemonade!

Knock-knock!

Who's there?

Les!

Les who?

Les party!

Knock-knock!

Who's there?

Les!

Les who?

Les face facts!

Knock-knock!

Who's there?

Les!

Les who?

Les is more!

Knock-knock!

Who's there?

Jess!

Jess who?

Jess the two of us!

**What kind of door
does a school of fish have?**

A stream door!

Ding Dong!

**What kind of door
does a living room have?**
A TV screen door!

Knock-knock!

Who's there?

Stu!

Stu who?

If the Stu fits, wear it!

Knock-knock!

Who's there?

Ray!

Ray who?

Ray-se the roof!

Knock-knock!

Who's there?

Rowan!

Rowan who?

Rowan wasn't built in a day!

222

Knock-knock!

Who's there?

Maura!

Maura who?

Maura the merrier!

Knock-knock!

Who's there?

Fritz!

Fritz who?

Fritz to be tied!

Knock-knock!

Who's there?

Sue!

Sue who?

Sue me!

Knock-knock!

Who's there?

Enid!

Enid who?

Enid you!

Knock-knock!

Who's there?

Ken!

Ken who?

Ken and bones!

Knock-knock!

Who's there?

Sela!

Sela who?

Sela with a kiss!

Knock-knock!

Who's there?

Granny!

Granny who?

Granny me a minute of your time!

Knock-knock!

Who's there?

Hedda!

Hedda who?

Hedda the sack!

Knock-knock!

Who's there?

Hedda!

Hedda who?

Hedda hurts—have-a an aspirin?

Answer The Door!

What kind of door is a haunted door?

A scream door!

CAN YOU GET THAT ?

What does a beaver's mom tell him when he goes out?

"Don't dam the door!"

Knock-knock!

Who's there?

Greta!

Greta who?

Greta minds think alike!

Knock-knock!

Who's there?

Bud!

Bud who?

Bud-der me up!

Knock-knock!

Who's there?

Fritz!

Fritz who?

Your refrigerator is on the Fritz! Help!

Knock-knock!

Who's there?

Hope!

Hope who?

Hope you're home!

Knock-knock!

Who's there?

Noah!

Noah who?

Noah problem!

Knock-knock!

Who's there?

Ray!

Ray who?

Ray of light!

Knock-knock!

Who's there?

Vera!

Vera who?

Vera, Vera has my little dog gone?

Ding Dong!

What does a goat's mom tell him when he goes out?

"Don't ram the door!"

Knock-knock!

Who's there?

Jay!

Jay who?

Jay L. Break!

Knock-knock!

Who's there?

Don Tootie!

Don Tootie who?

Don Tootie your own horn!

Knock-knock!

Who's there?

Bea!

Bea who?

Bea-m me up!

Knock-knock!

Who's there?

Ken!

Ken who?

Ken I come in?

What does a sweet potato's mom tell her when she goes out?
"Don't yam the door!"

Knock-knock!
Who's there?
Beth!
Beth who?
Beth my soul!

Knock-knock!
Who's there?
Dot!
Dot who?
Dot com!

Knock-knock!
Who's there?
Sol!
Sol who?
That's Sol, folks!

Knock-knock!

Who's there?

Fran!

Fran who?

Fran in need is a Fran indeed!

Knock-knock!

Who's there?

Kent!

Kent who?

Kent see you without my glasses!

238

Knock-knock!

Who's there?

Nan!

Nan who?

Nan of your business!

Knock-knock!

Who's there?

Claire!

Claire who?

Claire skies!

Knock-knock!

Who's there?

Stu!

Stu who?

Stu-dent driver!

Door Knobbies!

**What does a pig's mom
tell him when he goes out?**

"Don't ham the door!"

Answer The Door!

What does a shellfish's mom tell him when he goes out?
"Don't clam the door!"

Knock-knock!

Who's there?

Emma!

Emma who?

Emma late?

Knock-knock!

Who's there?

Lotta!

Lotta who?

Whole Lotta shakin' goin' on!

Knock-knock!

Who's there?

Lois!

Lois who?

Lois the opposite of high!

Knock-knock!

Who's there?

Laura!

Laura who?

Laura your music—you're keeping me awake!

Knock-knock!

Who's there?

Heinz!

Heinz who?

Heinz-sight!

Knock-knock!

Who's there?

Bjorn!

Bjorn who?

Bjorn free!

Knock-knock!

Who's there?

Denise!

Denise who?

Denise and Denephew!

Ding Dong!

What does a jelly doughnut's mom tell her when she goes out?

"Don't jam the door!"

Knock-knock!

Who's there?

Peggy!

Peggy who?

Peggy bank!

Knock-knock!

Who's there?

Ray!

Ray who?

No, Hoo-Ray!

Knock-knock!

Who's there?

Holly!

Holly who?

Holly-ween!

Knock-knock!

Who's there?

Pancho!

Pancho who?

Pancho lights out if you don't let me in!

Door Knobbies!

What does a sheep's mom tell him when he goes out?

"Don't lamb the door!"

Knock-knock!

Who's there?

Pearl!

Pearl who?

Pearl me a banana!

Knock-knock!

Who's there?

Penny!

Penny who?

Penny for your thoughts!

Knock-knock!

Who's there?

Plato!

Plato who?

Plato spaghetti!

Knock-knock!

Who's there?

Peephole!

Peephole who?

Peephole who live in glass houses shouldn't throw stones!

Knock-knock!

Who's there?

Bach!

Bach who?

Bach in five minutes!

248

Knock-knock!

Who's there?

Felon!

Felon who?

Felon the ice—you'll hear from my lawyer!

Knock-knock!

Who's there?

Theodore!

Theodore who?

Theodore? Now open it!

Knock-knock!

Who's there?

Nathan!

Nathan who?

Nathan to it!

Knock-knock!

Who's there?

Pierce!

Pierce who?

Pierce your ears!

Knock-knock!

Who's there?

Paolo!

Paolo who?

Paolo the leader!

Knock-knock!

Who's there?

Misty!

Misty who?

Misty bus—give me a ride!

Knock-knock!

Who's there?

Redford!

Redford who?

Redford is parked behind my car; can you move it?

What do you say when the doorbell doesn't smell?

"The doorbell is out of odor!"

Answer The Door!

**What do you call
it when you hang a coat on a door?**
Clothes-ing the door!

Knock-knock!

Who's there?

Richard!

Richard who?

Richard poor, will you still love me?

Knock-knock!

Who's there?

Darris!

Darris who?

Darris a train coming at two o'clock—be on it!

Knock-knock!

Who's there?

Sawyer!

Sawyer who?

Sawyer in half—I'm a magician!

252

Knock-knock!

Who's there?

Sean!

Sean who?

Let the sun Sean!

Knock-knock!

Who's there?

Regan!

Regan who?

Regan I don't know, cowboy!

Knock-knock!

Who's there?

Reuben!

Reuben who?

Reuben sandwich!

Knock-knock!

Who's there?

Rhonda!

Rhonda who?

Rhonda marathon!

Knock-knock!

Who's there?

Rocco 'n' Rollo!

Rocco 'n' Rollo who?

Rocco 'n' Rollo is here to stay!

**What do you call
it when you insult a door?**
Slamming the door!

Knock-knock!

Who's there?

Riona!

Riona who?

Riona car and a boat!

Knock-knock!

Who's there?

Rufus!

Rufus who?

Rufus leaking; do you want me to fix it?

Knock-knock!

Who's there?

Anita!

Anita who?

Anita hug!

Knock-knock!

Who's there?

Roger!

Roger who?

Roger! Over and out!

257

Knock-knock!

Who's there?

Roz!

Roz who?

Roz the flag!

Knock-knock!

Who's there?

Rob and Ruth!

Rob and Ruth who?

Ruth left—now it's just me, Rob. I'm Ruth-less.

Knock-knock!

Who's there?

Oliver!

Oliver who?

Oliver sudden I can't remember!

CAN YOU GET THAT?

**What do you call
a bullfighter's door?**
A mata-door!

Knock-knock!

Who's there?

Sadie!

Sadie who?

Sadie magic word!

Knock-knock!

Who's there?

Clara!

Clara who?

Clara-net is what I play in the band!

Knock-knock!

Who's there?

Walker!

Walker who?

Walker run—which should we do?

Knock-knock!

Who's there?

Forgetful!

Forgetful who?

Knock-knock!

Knock-knock!

Who's there?

Abbott!

Abbott who?

Abbott time you opened the door!

**What do you do on
a keyboard's doormat?**
Type your feet!

Knock-knock!

Who's there?

Adam!

Adam who?

Adam up and what do you get?

Knock-knock!

Who's there?

Alfredo!

Alfredo who?

Alfredo the Big Bad Wolf!

Knock-knock!

Who's there?

Ima!

Ima who?

Ima here to pick up your daughter!

263

Knock-knock!

Who's there?

Andy!

Andy who?

Andy winner is . . .

Knock-knock!

Who's there?

Scold!

Scold who?

Scold at the North Pole!

Knock-knock!

Who's there?

Anvil!

Anvil who?

Anvil you tell me your name too?

Knock-knock!

Who's there?

Atlas!

Atlas who?

Atlas someone wants to know all about me!

Ding Dong!

**What do you do
on an apple's doormat?**

Ripe your feet!

Knock-knock!

Who's there?

Leo!

Leo who?

Leo-dorant!

Knock-knock!

Who's there?

Apricot!

Apricot who?

Apricot my name!

Knock-knock!

Who's there?

Cereal!

Cereal who?

Cereal pleasure to meet you!

Knock-knock!

Who's there?

Hedda!

Hedda who?

Hedda the pack!

Knock-knock!

Who's there?

Perry!

Perry who?

Perry boat!

 **What do you do
on a plumber's doormat?**
Pipe your feet!

Knock-knock!

Who's there?

Candace!

Candace who?

Candace be true love?

Knock-knock!

Who's there?

Dina!

Dina who?

Dina's ready, wash up!

Knock-knock!

Who's there?

Cheese!

Cheese who?

Cheese the girl of my dreams!

269

Knock-knock!

Who's there?

Clancy!

Clancy who?

Clancy meeting you here!

Knock-knock!

Who's there?

Pigs!

Pigs who?

No, owls who; pigs oink!

Knock-knock!

Who's there?

Tennessee!

Tennessee who?

Tennessee sum of five plus five!

Knock-knock!

Who's there?

Mason!

Mason who?

Mason, my daughter, and me!

271

Knock-knock!

Who's there?

Dobie!

Dobie who?

Dobie cruel!

Knock-knock!

Who's there?

Idaho!

Idaho who?

Idaho—do you know?

Knock-knock!

Who's there?

Utah!

Utah who?

Utah too much!

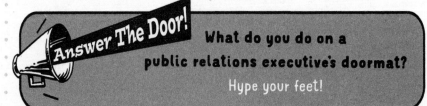

Answer The Door!

What do you do on a public relations executive's doormat?

Hype your feet!

Knock-knock!

Who's there?

Icy!

Icy who?

Icy London, Icy France, Icy your underpants!

Knock-knock!

Who's there?

Tish!

Tish who?

Tish upon a star!

What do you do on a complainer's doormat?
Gripe your feet!

Knock-knock!

Who's there?

Gwen!

Gwen who?

Gwen the moon hits your eye like a big pizza pie ...

Knock-knock!

Who's there?

Ethan!

Ethan who?

Ethan an apple a day keeps the doctor away!

Knock-knock!

Who's there?

Josie!

Josie who?

Josie Paris—it's beautiful this time of year!

Knock-knock!

Who's there?

Megan!

Megan who?

Megan a list, checkin' it twice!

Knock-knock!

Who's there?

Hera!

Hera who?

Hera comes the bride!

Knock-knock!

Who's there?

Irish!

Irish who?

Irish I knew!

 What does it sound like when you knock on a traffic signal's door?
Walk! Walk!

Knock-knock!

Who's there?

Jenny!

Jenny who?

Jenny old thing will do!

277

Knock-knock!

Who's there?

Sam!

Sam who?

Sam person who was knocking a minute ago!

Knock-knock!

Who's there?

Dwight!

Dwight who?

Dwight you are!

Knock-knock!

Who's there?

Ketchup!

Ketchup who?

Ketchup on all the latest gossip!

Knock-knock!

Who's there?

Kip!

Kip who?

Kip your eyes on your own paper!

CAN YOU GET THAT ?

**What does it sound like
when you knock on a locksmith's door?**
Lock! Lock!

Knock-knock!

Who's there?

Horace!

Horace who?

Horace sense!

Knock-knock!

Who's there?

Moose!

Moose who?

Moose likely to succeed!

Knock-knock!

Who's there?

Loki!

Loki who?

Loki before you leap-y!

Knock-knock!

Who's there?

Bess!

Bess who?

Bess personality!

281

Knock-knock!

Who's there?

Yul!

Yul who?

Yul be sorry!

Knock-knock!

Who's there?

Steven!

Steven who?

Steven I don't know the answer to that one!

Knock-knock!

Who's there?

Sari!

Sari who?

Sari—I really don't have a clue!

Knock-knock!

Who's there?

Patty O.!

Patty O. who?

Patty O. furniture!

Knock-knock!

Who's there?

Shirley!

Shirley who?

Shirley you jest!

Ding Dong!

What does it sound like when you knock on a parrot's door?
Talk! Talk!

What does it sound like when you knock on a foot's door?
Sock! Sock!

Knock-knock!

Who's there?

Tanya!

Tanya who?

Tanya speak up a bit?

Knock-knock!

Who's there?

Your mom!

Your mom who?

Very funny, now let me in!

Knock-knock!

Who's there?

Theresa!

Theresa who?

Theresa number that comes after two!

Knock-knock!

Who's there?

Betty!

Betty who?

Betty be on your toes!

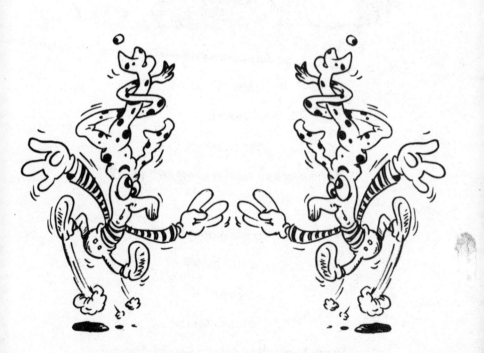

Knock-knock!

Who's there?

Vanna!

Vanna who?

Vanna make something out of it?

Knock-knock!

Who's there?

Juan!

Juan who?

Juan to wish you a happy birthday!

Knock-knock!

Who's there?

Wanda!

Wanda who?

Wanda go to the movies?

Knock-knock!

Who's there?

Yogurt!

Yogurt who?

Yogurt your way, and I'll go mine!

Knock-knock!

Who's there?

Dot!

Dot who?

Dot's all, folks!

Ding Dong!

What does it sound like when you knock on a boat's door?

Dock! Dock!

Craig Yoe has been an award-winning
creative director for Disney, Nickelodeon,
and the Muppets and looks funny.